Hayek, Currency Competition and European Monetary Union

Eighth Annual IEA Hayek Memorial Lecture

Given in London on Thursday, 27 May 1999

Professor Otmar Issing
Member of the Executive Board of the European Central Bank

With commentaries by

Professor Lawrence H. White
Professor Roland Vaubel

The IEA gratefully acknowledges the generous support of Deloitte & Touche for this annual lecture

Published by the Institute of Economic Affairs 2000

First published in March 2000 by
The Institute of Economic Affairs
2 Lord North Street
Westminster
London SW1P 3LB

© The Institute of Economic Affairs, 2000

Occasional Paper 111
All rights reserved
ISSN 0073-909X
ISBN 0-255 36481-4

Many IEA publications are translated into languages other than English
or are reprinted. Permission to translate or to reprint should be sought
from the General Director at the address above.

Printed in Great Britain by
Hartington Fine Arts Limited, Lancing, West Sussex
Set in Times Roman 11 on 13 point

Contents

[3]

Foreword

THE ANNUAL HAYEK MEMORIAL LECTURE is one of the principal events on the Institute's calendar. It is an occasion on which a major public figure addresses a large audience on an important topic. The 1999 Lecture was given by Professor Otmar Issing, who is a member of the Executive Board of the European Central Bank and was previously a Board Member of the Deutsche Bundesbank.

Professor Issing is not only an eminent monetary economist but one of Europe's most influential central bankers. He is also the author of two IEA papers[1] and has spoken on several occasions at Institute conferences. His lecture addressed one of Hayek's favourite themes – currency competition – which Professor Issing discussed in the context of European monetary union.

In summary, his argument is that adopting '... a Hayekian discovery process as a route to monetary union' would have been too risky. Nevertheless, '... a kind of Hayekian discovery process has ... been triggered by the introduction of the euro' which gives more scope for the private sector to '... enhance the quality of the medium-of-exchange and store-of-value functions of money'.

To encourage debate, the Institute usually publishes commentaries on the Hayek Lecture and an afterword by the lecturer. On this occasion, it asked two other distinguished economists to comment on Professor Issing's views – Professor Lawrence H. White of the University of Georgia and Professor Roland Vaubel of the University of Mannheim. Both commentators disagree with many of the points made by Professor Issing and, in general, with his contention that, in European monetary union, one can discern elements of a Hayekian discovery process. In his afterword, Professor Issing then discusses the criticisms made by Professors White and Vaubel.

---

[1] *Central Bank Independence and Monetary Stability*, Occasional Paper 89, 1993 and *Europe: Political Union through Common Money*, Occasional Paper 98, 1996.

All IEA publications contain the views of their authors, not those of the Institute (which has no corporate view), its Trustees, Advisers or Directors. The intention is to stimulate the discussion of significant topics and the expression of original ideas. That aim is amply fulfilled in Occasional Paper 111, given the high level of the debate it contains on the controversial issues raised by Professor Issing.

January 2000   COLIN ROBINSON
Editorial Director, Institute of Economic Affairs,
Professor of Economics, University of Surrey

The Authors

OTMAR ISSING, who was born in 1936, has been a member of the Executive Board of the European Central Bank since 1 June 1998. The business area for which he is responsible includes the Directorates General Economics and Research. Until May 1998 he was a Member of the Board of the Deutsche Bundesbank with a seat in the Central Bank Council. Prior to that he held Chairs of Economics at the Universities of Würzburg and Erlangen-Nürnberg. In 1991 he was awarded an honorary professorship at the University of Würzburg. From 1988 to 1990 he was a member of the Council of Experts for the Assessment of Overall Economic Developments. He is an active member of Akademie der Wissenschaften und der Literatur (Academy of Sciences and Literature), Mainz, and of the Academia Scientiarum et Artium Europaea (European Academy of Sciences and Arts). In addition to publishing numerous articles in scientific journals and periodicals, he is the author of, *inter alia*, two textbooks, namely *Einführung in die Geldtheorie* (Introduction to monetary theory), eleventh edition, 1998, and *Einführung in die Geldpolitic* (Introduction to monetary policy), sixth edition, 1996.

LAWRENCE H. WHITE is Professor of Economics in the Terry College of Business, University of Georgia, and Visiting Professor at the Queen's School of Management, Queen's University of Belfast. He is a member of the Academic Advisory Council of the IEA, and has recently been a visiting scholar at the Federal Reserve Bank of Atlanta. The views expressed here are his own and should not be attributed to any of these institutions. He is the author of *The Theory of Monetary Institutions* (Blackwell, 1999), *Free Banking in Britain* (2nd ed., IEA, 1995), and *Competition and Currency* (NYU Press, 1989). He is the editor of several works, including *The History of Gold and Silver* (3 vols., Pickering and Chatto, forthcoming), *The Crisis in American Banking* (NYU Press, 1993), and *Free Banking* (3 vols., Edward Elgar, 1993). His articles on monetary theory and banking history have appeared in a number of leading professional journals.

ROLAND VAUBEL is Professor of Economics at the University of Mannheim, Germany. He received a BA in Philosophy, Politics and Economics from the University of Oxford, an MA in economics from Columbia University, New York, and a doctorate in economics from the University of Kiel, Germany. He has been a researcher at the Institute of World Economics, University of Kiel (West Germany), Professor of Monetary Economics at Erasmus Universiteit, Rotterdam and Visiting Professor of International Economics at the University of Chicago (Graduate School of Business). He is a member of the Academic Advisory Council of the German Ministry of Economics and a member of the Academic Advisory Council of the Institute of Economic Affairs.

Professor Vaubel specialises in international finance, international organisations, public choice and social policy. His publications include *Strategies for Currency Unification. The Economics of Currency Competition and the Case for a European Parallel Currency* (1978); *The Political Economy of International Organisations* (1991), which he co-edited with Th.D. Willett; and *Political Competition, Innovation and Growth* (1998), which he coedited with Peter Bernholz and Manfred Streit. The IEA published his Wincott Memorial Lecture, *Choice in European Monetary Union* (IEA Occasional Paper No. 55, 1979) and his Hobart Paper 127, *The Centralisation of Western Europe (1995).*

Hayek, Currency Competition and European Monetary Union

Otmar Issing

1 Introduction

AS A YOUNG STUDENT I READ *THE ROAD TO SERFDOM*. It was the first book written by Hayek I came across, and it has left a deep and lasting influence on me. Only eleven years after the Hitler regime and the war I suddenly started to understand the interdependence between totalitarianism and economic policy. Since then I have read most of Hayek's publications. Many left their marks, although I will only mention here his impressive work *The Constitution of Liberty*.

But, perhaps more than anything else, it was the perception of 'competition as a discovery process' which has shaped my thinking. This approach is of the greatest relevance for economics, but goes far beyond this. Related to this 'discovery' is 'pretence of knowledge' as a permanent danger for societies. All those in public office responsible for making decisions should constantly bear this message in mind.

Against this background you can imagine that it is a great honour for me to be invited to give this lecture on the occasion of the 100th anniversary of Hayek's birth. Even more so as the invitation came from the Institute of Economic Affairs, an institution devoted to the study and propagation of liberal ideas – to the idea of liberty. I accepted immediately, despite the time constraints.

It was the Institute of Economic Affairs which in 1976 published Hayek's *Choice in Currency: A Way to Stop Inflation*. I chose the subject for my lecture for the following reasons. First of all because I might have some comparative advantage in a subject related to monetary economics. Having joined the Executive Board of the European Central Bank, Hayek's ideas on currency offer a special kind of interest. And, finally, it was the publication just mentioned which brought me in personal contact with Hayek. Fascinated (but, I may indicate already, not convinced) by the approach which was out of line with anything discussed in mainstream monetary theory at that time, I wished to include this paper in a reader on monetary policy issues I was preparing.

I proposed to preface the text with a quotation from Hayek: 'Inflation is made by government and its agents. Nobody else can do anything about it'. However, we could not agree on the translation of the word 'government' into German. After an extended correspondence we finally came to the conclusion in a telephone conversation that the quotation should remain, but in the original English.[1]

It only comes home to us fully how long and fruitful Hayek's career was when we realise that his rightly renowned monograph on the denationalisation of money was published some 60 years after his pioneering contribution to the theory of intertemporal equilibrium in *Weltwirtschaftliches Archiv*[2] in 1928. The monograph has to be seen against the background of decades of worldwide inflation. Hayek himself mentioned the great German inflation of 1923. After the Second World War, prices had moved worldwide in one direction only. In the course of the 1960s, 'booming' US Federal government expenditure, which was partly associated with the Vietnam War, led to a sustained period of strong growth in nominal aggregate demand. This, in turn, led to an increase in inflation in the US. In 1969 the inflation rate was already up to almost 6%, after having been less than 2% at the start of the decade. Given the Bretton Woods system of fixed exchange rates, the inflationary pressures emanating from the US spread out to other areas of the world, including Europe. The strain in the Bretton Woods system became apparent in the late 1960s. In 1973 the system finally collapsed. The problems created were magnified by the increase in oil and commodity prices in 1973. This led to soaring inflation.[3]

A few years later the industrial world was caught in a combination of high inflation and substantially increased unemployment. The policy that had brought the world to such an

---

[1] See Jürgen Badura und Otmar Issing, *Geldpolitik*, Stuttgart, 1980.

[2] 'Das intertemporale Gleichgewichtssystem der Preise und die Bewegungen des Geldwertes', which can be translated as 'The system of intertemporal price equilibrium and movements in the value of money'.

[3] See Michael Bruno and Jeffrey Sachs, *Economics of Worldwide Stagflation*, Harvard University Press, 1985, for an excellent description of this period.

unfavourable conjuncture, and that could be characterised by a belief that 'money does not matter' and a hubris of excessive reliance on demand management, had ostensibly failed. As Robert Lucas commented: 'This is the legacy of stagflation: a general loss of confidence, whether warranted or not, in the formerly accepted framework guiding discretionary economic management'.[4]

Hayek's view of these developments becomes clear from, for example, an excerpt from his Nobel Lecture, delivered in December 1974:

> Economists are, at this moment, called upon to say how to extricate the free world from the serious threat of accelerating inflation which, it must be admitted, has been brought about by policies that the majority of economists recommended or even urged governments to pursue. We have indeed at the moment little cause for pride: as a profession we made a mess of things.

He expanded on this in 1976:[5]

> practically all governments of history have used their exclusive power to issue money in order to defraud and plunder the people.

It was against this background that Hayek proposed his radical solution. It called for no less than the abolition of the government's monopoly over the issue of fiat money, leaving the way open for comprehensive competition in its supply by the private sector.

In his Hobart Paper Special No. 70, he spelt out his philosophy with respect to free competition in the supply of money:

> The purpose of this scheme is to impose upon existing monetary and financial agencies a very much needed discipline by making it impossible for any of them, or for any length of time, to issue a kind of money substantially less reliable and useful than the money of any other. As soon as the public became familiar with the new possibilities, any deviations from the straight path of providing an

---

4 Robert E. Jr. Lucas, 'Rules, Discretion and the Role of the Economic Advisor', in Stanley Fischer (ed.), *Rational Expectations and Economic Policy*, Chicago, 1980, p. 204.

5 *Choice in Currency: a Way to Stop Inflation*, IEA Occasional Paper 48, 1976.

honest money would at once lead to the rapid displacement of the offending currency by others. And the individual countries, being deprived of the various dodges by which they are now able temporarily to conceal the effects of their actions by 'protecting' their currency, would be constrained to keep the value of their currencies tolerably stable (p. 125).

Although his proposal was not implemented, his contribution kindled a lively and far-reaching debate on the role of government in the monetary system, a debate that addressed the choice between a free-market monetary regime and government management of the monetary system via a central bank. The proposal was so profound and radical in its conception that some leading advocates of a laissez-faire approach to most aspects of economic life (Milton Friedman, for example) were put on the defensive.

As it happened, Hayek also held some strong views on monetary union in Europe, an idea which was still only in a rather embryonic stage when he commented on it in 1978: his own scheme of competing currencies seemed to him

… both preferable and more practicable than the utopian scheme of introducing a new European currency, which would ultimately only have the effect of more deeply entrenching the source and root of all monetary evil, the government monopoly on the issue and control of money (p. 126).

2 Summary Presentation and Assessment of Hayek's Proposal for Competing Currencies

The proposal put forward by Hayek – that is, full competition between private issuers of currency – is an extremely interesting concept. It relates to the debate on the viability of unregulated banking and to the literature on the historical experience with free banking.[6]

---

[6] Hayek's proposal must be distinguished from free banking, which refers to a monetary system without a central bank, in which private banks would be allowed to issue currency and bank deposits without restriction. As practised in the 19th century, this version of free banking involved banknotes being redeemable in gold and silver coin (see Lawrence H. White, *Free Banking in Britain: Theory, Experience, and Debate*, 1800–1845, 2nd edn. IEA, 1995).

The basic idea seems to be as follows. Creating the possibility of banks issuing currency would open the way to competition. Banks could issue non-interest bearing certificates and open cheque accounts on the basis of their own distinct registered trade marks. Different banks would issue different certificates, in other words currencies. The currencies of different banks would trade at variable exchange rates. Competition and profit maximisation would lead to an equilibrium in which only banks paying a competitive return on liabilities could survive. Since currency corresponds here to non-interest-bearing certificates, the crucial requirement is the maintenance of the value of the currency. So, in equilibrium, only currencies guaranteeing a stable purchasing power would exist. Banks that failed to build up such a reputation for their currency would lose customers and be driven out of business.

Hayek was of the opinion that his proposal would, if implemented, contribute to the overall stability of the economy. In his monograph he wrote:

> The past instability of the market economy is the consequence of the exclusion of the most important regulator of the market mechanism, money, from itself being regulated by the market process.[7]

Let me now examine the characteristics of the equilibrium envisaged in Hayek's proposal.[8] The marginal costs of producing and issuing a currency (in the form of notes and coin) are rather low (close to zero).[9] In the context of the type of competition envisaged by Hayek, the nominal rate of interest would be driven (close) to zero. If the real rate of interest required by lenders to lend funds to borrowers were positive (say 3%), equilibrium in the loan market would require that lenders would have to be rewarded by a rate of deflation equal to this real rate. This would produce an outcome

---

[7] *Denationalisation of Money – the Argument Refined*, Hobart Paper Special No. 70, 2nd (extended) edn, IEA, 1978, p. 192.

[8] It should be noted that, in Hayek's proposal, equilibrium is assumed to exist and to be stable, and information is complete, symmetric and acquired at no cost. See Charles Goodhart, *The Evolution of Central Banks*, MIT Press, 1988.

[9] This is the assumption made by Milton Friedman in his seminal paper, 'The Optimum Quantity of Money' in *The Optimum Quanity of Money and other Essays*, Aldine, Chicago, 1969.

that has been advocated as a normative rule for inflation by Friedman in the past; that is, in a situation in which money is non-interest bearing, the optimal rate of inflation should be set equal to the negative of the real rate of interest. This is analogous, in this context, to the well-known correlation between free competition and efficiency (Pareto optimality).

Hayek's privatisation proposal would, initially at least, involve a multiplicity of privately issued moneys. If these failed to trade at par, which is not unlikely given that the financial health of the different issuers is likely to be different, then it is also likely that a multiplicity of exchange rates will also emerge between these privately issued currencies. So long as no restriction is imposed on the holding of the different currencies, those that are likely to depreciate in value would, according to Hayek's logic, be driven out of existence, leading to a situation in which only currencies with stable values would remain in existence.

Hayek believed that such competition between currencies was a discovery process, which would lead to a stable non-inflationary outcome. In this respect, it may be best to let Hayek speak for himself, which I do by quoting from his *Denationalisation of Money*:

> Indeed, if, as I am convinced, the main advantage of the market order is that prices will convey to the acting individuals the relevant information, only the constant observation of the course of current prices of particular commodities can provide information on the direction in which more or less money ought to be spent. Money is not a tool of policy that can achieve particular foreseeable results by control of its quantity. But it should be part of the self-steering mechanism by which individuals are constantly induced to adjust their activities to circumstances on which they have information only through the abstract signals of prices. It should be a serviceable link in the process that communicates the effects of events never wholly known to anybody and that is required to maintain an order in which the plans of participating persons match (pp. 192–3).

Nevertheless, despite Hayek's claims for this discovery process, most economists would argue that free competition with respect to money could not guarantee either a stable or an efficient outcome. This is the fundamental point.

In order to try to understand and assess Hayek's proposal, it is essential to take a closer look at money and its role in the economy. This is best done by, as it were, first breaking money up into its constituent functions. The classic textbook treatment of the functions of money is still valid. Money fulfils three functions:

- a unit of account
- a means of payment
- a store of value.

The use of money as a unit of account is, arguably, the most basic monetary function. It is the *numéraire*, that is the unit for quoting prices, for drawing funds, for negotiating contracts and for performing economic calculations. In this regard, money is a basic convention of society, such as the language and the standards of measurement. This seems to be a very Hayekian way of looking at money.

Indeed, the fundamental problem in economics for Hayek is that of co-ordinating the plans of many independent individuals. Competition through the market system leads to such a co-ordination. Individuals, acting in their own self-interest, respond to price signals. Prices, in turn, reflect the information available in society. Price signals allow the transmission of previously unknown information in the most synthetic and relevant way for the purpose of economic calculus. Now, prices – impersonal signals that provide for an extensive social division of labour – are expressed in terms of money. Irving Fisher coined the term 'money yardstick'.[10]

The unit of account represented by the respective unit of money (that is the euro, the US dollar, the Japanese yen, etc.) is a measuring tape or metric. With inflation or deflation, the metric keeps changing. The unit of account, as represented by money, becomes elastic and of uncertain dimension at any one time and of even more uncertain dimension over extended periods of time into the future. Inflation or deflation, therefore, means that the common unit-of-account language (or, say money language), for which the unit of account provides the foundations, is changing all the time.

---

[10] Irving Fisher, *The Money Illusion*, Adelphi, New York, 1928.

And uncertain inflation, which tends to accompany high inflation, means that the unit of account is changing in uncertain ways.

This impairs the efficiency of the common money language and, therefore, communication and co-ordination in the economy:

> Its undependability impairs the meeting of minds between borrowers and lenders and other transactors; it impairs economic calculation and co-ordination.[11]

One of these authors[12] invites his readers to

> consider how difficult constructing a house would be (ordering and fitting together the components, appliances, and all the rest) if the unit of length, the metre or the foot, kept changing and accordingly were perceived by different persons to have different sizes. Consider how preposterous it would be for the length of the metre to fluctuate according to supply and demand in the market for metre sticks. Yet our dollar suffers from a comparable absurdity – or a worse one, in view of the associated macroeconomic disorders.

Money used as a unit of account has characteristics of a public good. Given the unit-of-account function, the medium-of-exchange and store-of-value functions have traditionally, but not exclusively, been supplied by private enterprise.

Just as stable money is of crucial importance for a stable price level in a macroeconomic context, a stable price level is of equal significance for the efficient performance of money in a microeconomic context. A stable price level is, in principle, of central importance in ensuring that the three famous microeconomic functions which money provides are allowed to operate with maximum efficiency.[13] From the point of view of the public

---

[11] See R. Greenfield and L. Yeager (1983), 'A Laissez-Faire Approach to Monetary Stability', *Journal of Money, Credit and Banking*, Vol. 15, pp. 302–15.

[12] L. Yeager (1983), 'Stable Money and Free Market Currencies', Cato Journal, Vol. 3, No. 1, pp. 305–26.

[13] As is well known by now, the Governing Council of the ECB has not opted for strict price stability as an objective but has rather defined price stability '... as a year-on-year increase in the Harmonised Index of Consumer Prices (HIPC) for the euro area of below 2%'. Price stability, according to this definition, 'is to be maintained over the medium term'.

involvement in the economy, the unit of account is of the greatest importance.

Efficient co-ordination in the economy cannot occur unless the various agents involved (that is, virtually everybody) speak the same money language. The institution that allows them to do so is money itself, but more specifically the unit-of-account function of money. The decentralised plans of hundreds of millions of consumers and millions of producers and distributors cannot mesh harmoniously in the aggregate if this common money language, as encapsulated in the unit-of-account function of money, is missing. The efficiency of this language in performing this vital co-ordination role depends crucially on whether the unit of account always means the same thing to different individuals both at one and the same moment and over time. A necessary condition for it to mean the same thing is that price stability prevails both at any moment in time and with a credible commitment that it will continue to prevail into the indefinite future. From this point of view, the commitment to maintaining price stability is like the standardisation of units of measurement.

It is not difficult to imagine problems in the Hayek proposal arising from the inherent dynamics behind the discovery process, which would characterise competition between banks in the supply of currency. There are many questions left unanswered by Hayek about how the discovery process would work in practice. How would the economy function during this discovery process? Since bad issuers are, according to the theory, driven out by the fact that they have recourse to inflationary issuance, this suggests that the discovery process would itself be characterised by inflation. Furthermore, if, say, a single stable currency did initially emerge from the discovery process, how could one be sure that, having established a monopoly, the private issuer would not then, in a time-inconsistent fashion that has become all too familiar under politically dependent central banks, start to engage in inflationary over-issue so as to maximise seigniorage? And even if a few issuers were to survive, how could one be sure that the resulting oligopoly situation would not result in collusion or instabilities?

Another potential problem with the Hayek proposal is that the real rate of interest would tend to vary across the business cycle in response to the short-run pressures of supply and demand for loans and so too, according to his scheme, would the rate of deflation. And, of course, a steady rate of deflation would only emerge if the whole private sector discovery process is itself stable, which any reasonable person might be permitted to doubt. It would therefore appear that the outcome earnestly desired by Hayek, a money of stable value, would not be achieved in practice by his own proposal of competing currencies.

In a situation in which money were to be issued by many different issuers as in Hayek's proposal and, either because of over-issuing by some agents or because of poor investment decisions, these issues failed to trade at parity, then many different *numéraires* could emerge. In principle, there could, in the end, be as many *numéraires* as there are issuers. In the presence of many *numéraires* or, more meaningfully, in the absence of a single *numéraire*, financial communication, based on the common money language which would be provided by a single *numéraire*, would degenerate. This would probably result in very poor co-ordination in the economy, with the efficiency of the decentralised decision-making of firms and households, which is the hallmark of capitalist economies, being jeopardised and the productive potential of the economy being gravely endangered. The purely private provision of a public good (the unit-of-account function of money) would, in this case, be sub-optimal since private issuers cannot easily underpin the single *numéraire*. Nor do they have an incentive to do so since they cannot capture the vast social benefits of the common monetary language provided by the unit-of-account function of money.

There are further issues that any proposal in the spirit of Hayek would have to confront. First, the use of money in transactions makes it subject to network externalities. Network externalities, in turn, may inhibit free competition and may make it difficult, if not impossible, to dislodge an incumbent issuer who has resorted to inflationary issuance. In other words, networking externalities would inhibit Hayek's discovery process from working as he envisaged it. Network externalities also provide a rationale for regulation. Second, the assumption of complete, symmetric and free information implicitly assumed in the Hayek proposal does not apply to banking. The remark is equally valid in terms of banking activities (for example, a fundamental activity in banking is the evaluation of the creditworthiness of borrowers) and banks themselves (the special nature of the balance sheets of banks makes their valuation and risk assessment particularly difficult). In the absence of symmetric information, important issues of moral hazard, adverse selection and systemic stability become relevant.[14]

Networking externalities therefore mean that there is no guarantee that new entrants into the market for supplying money would be able to dislodge the incumbent issuer(s) if they resorted to inflationary issuance, given the inertia that is an inherent part of phenomena subject to networking effects such as currencies. In any case, why should people be willing to believe the claims of any potential new entrant that its currency will, unlike that of the incumbent(s), turn out to be stable? In my opinion, there are too many unanswered questions for Hayek's proposal for currency competition to be a viable candidate for society searching for a stable monetary system.

Furthermore, it is very unlikely that the kind of uncertainty about future prices, which Hayek wanted to banish with his proposal ('… a money of stable value is really the best we can hope for'), would be the outcome if his proposal were to be implemented. Hayek's discovery process could, on the contrary, entail substantial costs in practice. According to his own logic of free competition in privately issued currencies, the nominal interest rate would be driven to zero with, as already explained, deflation being the outcome. Hayek's proposal would not therefore deliver what it seems to promise, namely price stability. Under his proposal, there would still be uncertainty about the future price level.

3 Hayek and Gresham's Law

Under Hayek's scheme, market forces would determine the relative values of the different competing currencies. In other words, the exchange rates between the competing currencies would float freely. People would not want to hold on to the currency of an issuer that was expected to depreciate relative to one that was expected to hold its value in terms of purchasing power over

---

[14] See, for example, Goodhart, *op. cit.*

goods and services. Therefore, good money that maintained its purchasing power would drive out the depreciation- and inflation-prone bad money. However, it is not inconceivable that competing private issuers would decide to collude by fixing the relative values of their currencies. They would do this by agreeing to intervene mutually whenever any of the currencies in question came under pressure in the market for these currencies. This would be easier to do, and would be more likely to succeed, if there were only a few issuers left after the Hayekian discovery process had reached some equilibrium state.

Although this could be the outcome in a Hayek world of competing private currencies, it would clearly not be appreciated by Hayek himself. This is because, if some arrangement were to be arrived at by private issuers to counter the tendency for the values of the different moneys to fluctuate against each other, then the bad money would begin to drive out the good money, the exact opposite of what Hayek himself espoused. In other words, Gresham's law would, most likely, start to apply.

As Hayek himself put it:

If the law makes two kinds of money perfect substitutes for the payment of debts and forces creditors to accept a coin of smaller content of gold in the place of one with a larger content, debtors will, of course, pay only in the former and find a more profitable use for the substance of the latter.[15]

And:

(Gresham's Law) is not false, but it applies only if a *fixed rate of exchange* between the different forms of money is enforced [italics in original].[16]

The bad money (over-issued and inflation-prone) would start to drive out the good money (well-managed and maintaining stable purchasing power). More of the bad money would be produced at the expense of the good money and inflation would accelerate.

---

[15] See *Denationalisation of Money, op. cit.*, p. 142.

[16] *ibid.*

In principle, Hayek's proposal also works with national currencies produced monopolistically by central banks provided the
currencies in question are convertible and can be freely exchanged
against each other on foreign exchange markets. In such settings,
good national currencies will tend to increase in importance relative to bad, inflation-prone, national currencies. This naturally
constrains the ability of national governments to use 'their exclusive power to issue money in order to defraud and plunder the
people.'[17] In this context, I think it is fair to say that the widespread
use of the Deutschmark, for example, as an international investment
currency is symptomatic of the enduring success of the Bundesbank
in maintaining, in relative terms, the internal purchasing power of
the Deutschmark. However, as long as national currencies remain
legal tender only within their own national boundaries, the scope
for good national currencies to drive out bad national currencies
may not be as complete as in the Hayekian world of competing
private currencies where none of these currencies has the status of
legal tender. In other words, Hayek's competition between
currencies goes beyond the limited competition we have seen on
foreign exchange markets between national currencies.

If this limited competition between national currencies is
insufficient to constrain domestic monetary policy to refrain from
excessive monetary creation, then a government may decide to
tie its hands further by opting for a currency board arrangement.
This would eliminate the possibility of any discretionary domestic
monetary policy action since the domestic component of the monetary base could only change in response to a change in the foreign
currency component of the base. Our experience with the currency
board arrangement to date is limited, but nevertheless allows us to
declare it, provisionally, to be a success.

Some governments that have opted for this arrangement have
found, however, that during the recent financial market turbulence,
their economies were not immune from contagious spillover
despite having fairly healthy economic fundamentals. This is the
result of the currency board arrangement not being an unequivocal
one since the government in question retains the option of revoking

---

[17] *ibid.*

the arrangement. Financial markets will therefore factor this possibility into their calculations and actions, ensuring that these countries suffer some contagious effects. This has stimulated a debate as to whether it would not be better for such currency board countries to go beyond the currency board arrangement and opt for full 'dollarisation' (see below).

Hayek espoused the denationalisation of currencies. He recommended that this be achieved through a comprehensive privatisation of the supply of money. It is notable that, of the two routes to denationalisation of currencies that have been taken so far, neither follows the route recommended by Hayek. One is the route taken by the governments of the Euro 11[18] through an international agreement of equals, which has resulted in the arrival of the euro. Another route is through what is known as 'dollarisation' whereby a country voluntarily relinquishes its own currency in favour of adopting a foreign currency, the 'dollar'.

It appears to me, therefore, that under the Hayek proposal, we are likely to reach either one or other of the following unfavourable outcomes.

- On the one hand, we could see the emergence of floating exchange rates between different privately issued moneys, resulting in an uncertain discovery process without any guarantee of a stable outcome, along with a deterioration in economic communication and co-ordination in the economy overall.
- On the other hand, any attempt by private issuers to pre-empt these outcomes by fixing the exchange rates between their currencies would probably trigger Gresham's law and result in accelerating inflation.

4 The Importance of Inside Money

Since the birth of central banking, governments – via the central bank – have supplied financial instruments that have simultaneously

---

18 The participating countries of the Eurosystem, known as the Euro 11, are Austria, Belgium, Finland, France, Germany, Ireland, Italy, Luxembourg, the Netherlands, Portugal and Spain.

fulfilled all of the three functions of money I have already mentioned. They have suppressed competition in the supply of currency and bank reserves (that is, so-called *outside money*). However, they have not suppressed competition in the supply of the other components of money, that is so-called *inside money*, which has been supplied exclusively by the private sector. Until quite recently, inside money consisted exclusively of bank deposits which were supplied competitively by banks. However, governments have nevertheless restricted the supply of means of payment and stores of value by the private sector in the past, although this has been very substantially liberalised over the last twenty years or so. The result is that the availability of efficient means of payment that can also serve as good stores of value (and thus as a hedge against inflation) has improved almost beyond recognition compared with what was available during the period of financial repression.

Although governments have retained a monopoly on the production of high-powered money, they have always permitted and indeed increasingly encouraged competition in the production of inside money. The upshot of this is that outside money now comprises only a rather small fraction of total money balances (taking, say, a broad definition of the money stock). After undergoing a dramatic decline, particularly in the period following the Second World War, it now ranges from about 1% in the US and about 5% in the United Kingdom to about 6% in Germany.[19] There are very good reasons for the government monopoly over the production of high-powered money. Notes and coin issued by the central bank and, in some cases, by the government are unique in the following sense: they are the only instrument that can mediate a transaction and settle it with finality at one and the same time, by virtue of their status as legal tender. Currency is also unique in that it supplies the unit of account for the whole economy.

Although privately supplied inside money and publicly supplied outside money compete with one another as transaction media and

---

[19] Both the US and German figures are corrected for estimated holdings of dollar and Deutsche Mark currency held outside the US and Germany respectively.

stores of value, there is nevertheless a kind of symbiotic relationship between the two for two reasons:

- Inside money (predominantly bank deposits) may owe its acceptability to the fact that its issuers promise, and indeed are legally bound, to redeem it in outside money.[20]
- Outside money provides the unit of account for the whole system, without which inside money might be less acceptable in the absence of a single (commodity) *numéraire*.

Seen in this light, it appears that Hayek was correct in arguing that efficiency and (price) stability would be enhanced if money were to be supplied privately and competitively. Indeed, the fact is that most of our conventionally measured money stocks are now composed predominantly of inside money, that is, money supplied by private enterprise, but more specifically the medium-of-exchange and store-of-value functions of this inside money. Hayek's arguments for free competition in the supply of money are therefore, in principle, applicable to these two functions of inside money. However, I believe he was mistaken in thinking that the economy would best be served if his recommendation were to apply to all aspects or functions of money. His recommendation neglected the 'public good' aspect of money, which derives from its function as a unit of account. Money with a stable purchasing power serves as the universally acceptable unit of account even for agents who do not use it as a medium of exchange or a store of value.

It could be argued that, with monetary union in Europe, two things have happened which play a role in the current discussion.

- The geographical reach of the new unit of account, the euro, has been extended dramatically, relative to that of its forerunner currencies (or forerunner units of account).
- The degree of competition between private sector agents in the provision of the other two functions of money, as a medium of exchange and a store of value, will almost certainly be enhanced,

---

[20] Either immediately (sight deposits), upon maturity (time deposits) or after a period of notice (savings deposits).

leading – over time – to considerable improvements in the quality of the latter.

The introduction of the new single unit of account means that there has, as from the beginning of January 1999, already been a direct and immediate welfare gain for both producers and consumers since the 'moneyness' of existing money balances has been greatly enhanced. There are several sources of this welfare gain. To mention just one: the merger of the currencies of the Euro 11 countries into the single currency, the euro, in January 1999 has – in one fell swoop – eliminated foreign exchange transaction costs for all cross-border transactions within the euro area.

Indeed, it is because of the greatly extended reach of the new single unit of account that the scope available to the private sector to improve the quality of money has been greatly enhanced. This will operate through the new competitive opportunities for the banking and financial industries in the whole euro area. Welfare will be further enhanced over time as the single currency imparts the necessary critical mass to the single money and financial services market in Europe.

5 Hayek Transposed into the World of the New Payment Technologies and e-money

Hayek's analysis and comments related to a world of what might be called *analogue money*, that is money that was represented as book entries (bank deposits, or inside money) or in the form of paper notes or metal coin (outside money). Despite the fact that many earlier predictions of the demise of paper money have turned out to be false, I think it is safe to say that it is at last making way for the ongoing digital revolution as reflected in the dramatic progress in computer and communications technologies. These developments are now underpinning rapid advances in payment and settlement infrastructures. This has enabled new payment media to emerge that compete directly with the means of payment, that is notes and coin, issued by the central bank and backed by government. New payment media take many forms, but the most commonly known are prepaid cards (e-money) and debit cards. Still more advanced forms of digital money, such as electronic network money (cybermoney), have now become technically feasible and may soon make their commercial appearance. These present new opportunities for a much more efficient payment system, but at the same time pose new challenges for monetary arrangements and monetary policy.

An aspect worth emphasising here is the fact that central bank money in the form of notes and coin does not need a payments infrastructure in order to mediate payments. As has already been noted, central bank money can perform the payment and settlement functions (with finality) at one and the same time, by virtue of its legal tender status. However, privately issued financial instruments (bank deposits, for example) are not money in this sense unless complemented by a payments infrastructure. The analogue payments structures with which we have become so familiar in many countries are cheques and cheque clearing. The payments technologies now becoming available to the private sector are undergoing unprecedented improvements. The effects are likely to be profound. Their widespread application could eventually mean radical rethinking about what we understand by money. In particular, they will increasingly provide private enterprise with far greater scope to compete directly with central bank notes and coin as payment media.

There is a very specific part of this process which deserves special attention. When there is a delay between a transaction and its settlement, as is the case in most existing privately supplied paper-based payment and settlement infrastructures (using cheques and paper-based direct debits, for example), there is an element of risk attached to most of the payments effected in this way. A number of different types of risk are involved – for example, credit risk, interest rate risk and operational risk. The risks involved in these privately based payments media imparted a comparative advantage to currency as a transaction medium, since the latter was the only instrument that could perform a payment and settlement function (with finality) at one and the same time, by virtue of its legal tender status. This meant that notes and coin facilitated transactions in anonymous market situations since the seller never had to worry about the creditworthiness of the buyer.

However, an important feature of the new electronic payment and settlement infrastructure is its ability (at least potentially) to compress the transactions–settlement time lag to what is virtually zero in economic time. This creates an essentially new situation which has the potential to obviate many, if not all, of the types of risk normally encountered in executing payments and their settlement with inside money and, in principle, allows a much wider array of assets, especially marketable assets, to be mobilised as transaction media. The new technology allows the vendor to verify that the purchaser possesses sufficient funds to cover the transaction and, in principle, permits a transfer of these funds to the vendor's bank account in real time. It further allows the vendor to verify in real time that the funds have indeed been credited to his or her account. This allows the settlement of the transaction with finality to occur at virtually the same time as the transaction itself.

Privately supplied payment instruments therefore now have the potential, when complemented with the most up-to-date computer and communications technologies, to provide a more attractive alternative to notes and coin as a transaction medium. And, given that the former are also potentially much more efficient in a number of ways, it is not inconceivable that one could face the prospect of a rapid erosion of the role of notes and coin as transaction media in the not-too-distant future.

The type of networking effects that support the acceptance of the euro are the same as those supporting the growth of electronic competition to notes and coin. More specifically, the price people are *willing* to pay for the use of electronic means of payment increases with the number of existing users (demand-side economies of scale), whereas the price they would *have* to pay is likely to fall as a result of declining unit costs of production as output expands (supply-side economies of scale, which tend to be large for networking products) and as competition forces lower costs to be passed on to customers. This dynamic would, of course, only start to take effect once a critical mass of usage has been attained.

There may also be forces promoting the growth of electronic means of payment at work which are unique to the euro area and the changeover process to stage 3B of economic and monetary union. In the case of the euro, the conventional channels of access to a currency at the retail level (notes and coins) will not be available for the first three years, i.e. throughout stage 3A of monetary union. The only means of access to the euro for households, and possibly for many small firms, may therefore be via electronic media, both electronic money and electronic access products that allow scriptural money (bank deposits) denominated in euro to be mobilised for transaction purposes. The non-availability of the euro in the form of notes and coins could therefore impart an extra stimulus to the growth of e-money and electronic access products.

The assumption from the current perspective is that all of these new payment instruments will be issued by private issuers. Despite fairly extensive discussions of the topic among central bankers, there has been no suggestion that central banks should issue e-money or be involved in the new retail electronic payments infrastructure as an active participant. Therefore, the growth of electronic means of payment will amount to an important further step in the process of privatisation in the field of the payments and monetary system, especially because the new digital payment media compete directly with the analogue-based media (notes and coins) supplied by the central bank. If this were to happen to such an extent that central bank money were driven out of the business of retail payments, then Hayek's vision would almost have been achieved[21] – but with two distinct differences:

- it would have been achieved by a gradual evolution in financial market innovation and by improvements in payment technologies, rather than by the type of top-down legislative decree that Hayek himself had envisaged to remove the central bank entirely from monetary management.
- that evolution would have occurred without jeopardising the single unit of account.

This gradual process of privatisation is one which central banks might logically be expected to oppose, but they have not. On the contrary, they are actively taking steps to help promote the growth of electronic substitutes for notes and coins. They are doing so by seeking agreement between the competent official bodies and potential private sector issuers on standardisation – the objective being to promote inter-operability between different privately supplied alternatives. Although this might seem like the proverbial

---

[21] Central bank money could, of course, remain as a transactions and settlement medium at the wholesale level in the interbank market.

turkeys voting for Christmas, central bankers place a very high priority on the smooth and efficient working of the payment system at both the retail and wholesale levels.

The European Central Bank (ECB) therefore considers it essential that the following minimum requirements be fulfilled:

- issuers of electronic money must be subject to prudential supervision;
- the issuance must be subject to sound and transparent legal arrangements, technical security, protection against criminal abuse and monetary statistics reporting;
- issuers of electronic money must be legally obliged, at the request of the holders, to redeem electronic money against central bank money at par; and
- the possibility must exist for central banks to impose reserve requirements on all issuers of electronic money.

The ECB has also identified two further objectives, the pursuit of which it deems to be desirable: the inter-operability of electronic money schemes and the adoption of adequate guarantee, insurance or loss-sharing schemes to protect depositors. The third requirement mentioned is of particular significance in the context of the current discussion. This is because, from a monetary policy point of view,

> the redeemability requirement is, *inter alia*, necessary in order to preserve the unit-of-account function of money, to maintain price stability by avoiding any unconstrained issuance of electronic money, and to safeguard the controllability of the liquidity conditions and short-term interest rates set by the ESCB.[22]

If the whole process triggered by the availability of new electronic retail means of payment is finally brought to its logical conclusion, as suggested by the dynamics of technological development and free competition, central banks and governments will be confronted with a very specific problem of pivotal significance: can the unit of account be separated from the means of payment, while still remaining a viable unit of account and playing the

---

[22] *ECB Annual Report*, 1998, p. 106.

crucial role of providing the common money language for the whole economy? If the means of payment embodying the unit of account, that is notes and coins, is – over time – eliminated as a transaction medium by virtue of the competition of the emerging digital equivalents issued by the private sector, would the familiar existing units of account such as the euro, the US dollar and the pound sterling, continue to mean anything? And, if not, what should be the official response? I do not propose to address either of these issues in this paper, but you may rest assured that they are crucial to our concerns for the future, albeit probably the somewhat distant future.

Hayek seems to have had very little doubt but that private enterprise, operating in a largely unregulated environment, would deliver a monetary system that is stable, safe and efficient. However, I remain rather sceptical whether the private sector can cope with all the externalities involved in the provision of a smoothly working monetary and financial system. It must nevertheless be conceded that the private sector is increasingly helping to evolve a monetary and financial system, supported by increasingly sophisticated payments infrastructures, that promises to be significantly more efficient than the system it is gradually displacing. There is, accordingly, no strong case to be made for attempting to introduce such a system by fiat. It is preferable that it should evolve by piecemeal engineering, rather than by some abrupt legislative change as sought by proponents of competing currencies and free banking, of which Hayek could, with some justification, be regarded as the high priest. It should also be borne in mind that, during this transitional period and afterwards, the central bank will continue to play an important role as a regulator of the financial system by, *inter alia*, setting the rules for competition between private suppliers of inside money.

6 Hayek's Legacy and Monetary Union

Hayek referred in 1978 (*op. cit.*) to the possibility of monetary union in clear and strong terms. He put it like this:

> though I strongly sympathise with the desire to complete the economic unification of Western Europe by completely freeing the flow of money between them, I have grave doubts about doing so by creating a new European currency managed by any sort of supranational authority. Quite apart from the extreme unlikelihood that

the member countries would agree on the policy to be pursued in practice by a common monetary authority (and the practical inevitability of some countries getting a worse currency than they have now), it seems highly unlikely that it would be better administered than the present national currencies.

At one level, monetary union encompassing the Euro 11 countries could, therefore, be seen as a project diametrically opposed to the type of scheme advocated by Hayek in the passages I have quoted. Instead of allowing the private sector to compete in issuing its own currencies, the single currency was introduced by governments coming together and introducing the euro in a top-down fashion by legislative decree, while continuing to prohibit the private sector from issuing currency. Any attempt by the private sector to issue banknotes or coins is counterfeiting, a serious criminal offence.

At another level, one can see many strands in Hayek's thinking that may have influenced the course of the events leading to monetary union in subtle ways. What has happened with the introduction of the euro has indeed achieved the denationalisation of money, as advocated by Hayek, at least in the Euro 11 countries. Furthermore, the euro is being managed by a central bank (the ECB) that is protected from political interference by a treaty (the Maastricht Treaty), to which all Member States are signatories. All national central banks that comprise the Eurosystem are now independent of their respective Euro 11 governments and, according to their respective statutes, cannot take instructions from these governments.

Moreover, the Eurosystem is supranational and does not therefore have any natural political counterpart in the form of a supranational government with full executive powers. This further underpins the independence of the Eurosystem and enables it to pursue its mandated ultimate objective, that is price stability, without interference from government. Thus, monetary policy in the Euro 11 countries has been denationalised and is being conducted by a supranational central bank, which is politically independent of the governments of the Member States. Furthermore, any monetary financing of the public sector or privileged access to financial institutions is prohibited. The separation between public finance and monetary policy is thereby ensured.

This is very much in line with views expressed by Hayek:[23]

It may still be true that, if there were full agreement as to what monetary policy ought to aim for, an independent authority fully protected against political pressure and free to decide on the means to be employed in order to achieve the ends it has been assigned might be the best arrangement. The old argument in favour of independent central banks still has great merit.

He goes on to elaborate that

under present conditions we have little choice but to limit monetary policy by prescribing its goals rather than its specific actions.

He then comments on employment and price stability as goals for monetary policy, concluding that

the two aims are not necessarily in conflict provided that the requirements for monetary stability are given first place and the rest of economic policy is adapted to them.

Last, but not least, Hayek emphasised (again strongly) the dangers from monetary financing:

if we are to preserve a functioning market economy, *nothing can be more urgent than that we dissolve the unholy marriage between monetary and fiscal policy*, long clandestine, but formally consecrated with the victory of Keynesian economics. [italics in original][24]

7 Conclusions

Hayek himself has explained the objectives of his proposal:

the abolition of the government monopoly of money was conceived to prevent the bouts of acute inflation and deflation, which plagued the world for the last sixty years.

---

[23] Friedrich A. von Hayek, *The Constitution of Liberty*, Routledge, London, 1960.

[24] Friedrich A. von Hayek, 1978, *op. cit.*

Hayek was very clear about where to put the blame:

> the basic tools of civilisation – language, morals, law and money –
> are all results of spontaneous growth and not of design, and of the
> last two organised power has got hold and thoroughly corrupted
> them.[25]

Or, as he put it later, in even stronger terms:

> the history of government management of money has, except for a
> few happy periods, been one of incessant fraud and deception.[26]

The institutional reform which he espoused to tackle this problem was indeed radical. It involved, as we have seen, the denationalisation of money to be achieved by the abolition of the government's monopoly over the issue of fiat money leaving the way open for supply of money to be determined by comprehensive private sector competition.

I would not be doing justice to Hayek if I neglected to mention that, at an earlier stage in his thinking, he put forward proposals for controlling inflation which have now become the conventional wisdom. In Chapter 21 of his famous book *The Constitution of Liberty* (1960), he wonders, as I have just indicated, whether an independent monetary authority, fully protected against political pressure and free to decide on the means to be employed in order to achieve the ends it has been assigned, might be the best arrangement.

However, he seems to have viewed central bank independence as an inadequate solution since, as early as the 1960s, he concluded, in light of the high level of government debt, that

> … an effective monetary policy can be conducted only in co-
> ordination with the financial policy of the government. Co-ordination
> in this respect, however, inevitably means that whatever nominally

---

[25] Friedrich A. von Hayek, *Law, Legislation and Liberty*, University of Chicago Press, 1979.

[26] Friedrich A. von Hayek, *The Fatal Conceit: the Errors of Socialism*, Routledge, London, 1988.

independent monetary authorities still exist have in fact to adjust their policy to that of the government.[27]

I think it is now clear that it was ideas along these lines that were the inspiration behind the rules and procedures in the EU Treaty, and I refer in particular to Articles 104 and 104a. In fact, I would argue that one reason for Hayek's change of mind and his subsequent advocacy of complete privatisation of money, as revealed by the views expressed in *The Constitution of Liberty* in 1960 and those put forward in *The Denationalisation of Money* in 1978, is to be found in his disappointment with the trends in the monetary institutions during his lifetime. He seems to have said as much:

> ... high hopes of what could be expected from political control over money have been bitterly disappointed. ... *unchecked party politics and stable money are inherently incompatible* [italics in the original].[28]

The tentative answer to Hayek's concern – the now classic inflation bias induced by time inconsistency – was finally found in institutional reform. In all industrialised countries monetary policy is now being managed by (more or less) independent central banks with the key objective of maintaining price stability. Monetary financing of the public sector is excluded. Monetary stability is protected by law and social consensus.

If Hayek were alive today, how would he see EMU and the ECB? Let me hazard what is probably a somewhat biased and speculative answer. The route to monetary union taken by member governments and central banks was almost diametrically opposed to that espoused by him in his later writings. But should he not welcome what we have achieved? Should he not be pleased that so much of his earlier (1960) blueprint is now law?

I am convinced that he would welcome the fact that the ECB has not joined the new fashionable wave arguing that money does not

[27] See Hayek, 1960, *op. cit.*, p. 327.

[28] Friedrich A. von Hayek, 'Market Standards for Money', *Economic Affairs*, April–May 1986.

matter. It is very easy to slip into the trap of thinking that money is unimportant when inflation is low and to ignore the overwhelming evidence that all past episodes of persistent inflation have been preceded, or been accompanied, by rapid money growth. Robert Lucas in his Nobel Lecture has only recently reminded us of the facts, and I quote:

> ... the prediction that prices respond proportionately to changes in money in the long run, deduced by Hume in 1752 (and by many other theorists, by many different routes, since), has received ample – I would say decisive – confirmation, in data from many times and places.[29]

As I have already argued, the quality of money, which has to do with how well it performs its micro-economic functions of medium of exchange, store of value and in particular unit of account, is related to the quantity of money. Too much of the latter, relative to *ex ante* demand for money, can substantially impair the former. Since inflation is ultimately a monetary phenomenon, money constitutes a natural, firm and reliable 'nominal anchor' for a monetary policy aimed at price stability. This accounts for why money is given a prominent role in the ECB's monetary policy strategy.

Therefore, although the path taken to achieve denationalisation of money has been very different from that advocated by Hayek, the ultimate objective that he sought – monetary independence from political interference and price stability – has, to all intents and purposes, already been achieved. Of course, I should add as an essential precautionary note that price stability is never fully achieved in the sense that it is a forward-looking concept; the ECB must be eternally vigilant, and act in a pre-emptive way, to ensure that inflationary pressures are not given an opportunity to translate into actual inflation. Having said this, however, I am afraid Hayek might not be in favour of a new centralised authority with monopoly powers over base money. The Treaty of Maastricht is virtually the very opposite of what Hayek proposed, because, among other

---

[29] Robert E. Lucas, Jr., 'Nobel Lecture: Monetary Neutrality', *Journal of Political Economy*, Vol. 104, No. 4, 1996, p. 668.

things, the new monetary order in the Euro 11 has been created not in an evolutionary process but in a 'constructivist' way by statute at a fixed date (1 January 1999).

I am convinced that the Euro 11 governments have, in principle, taken the correct route to monetary union. They could hardly afford to take what might have been an enormous risk in adopting a Hayekian discovery process as a route to monetary union, as had been advocated in the so-called hard ECU proposal.[30] This would amount to experimenting with the monetary constitution, a very dangerous strategy. Continuity in monetary arrangements and institutions is of the essence. A premium must be placed on the tried and tested. It is therefore preferable to subscribe to a philosophy of piecemeal engineering in the reform of a proven monetary system by allowing it to evolve in response to the needs of the economy and to the opportunities provided by advances in technology in an efficient fashion.

Although the hard currency proposal has not been adopted, and correctly so in my view, it could nevertheless be plausibly argued that a kind of Hayekian discovery process has indeed been triggered by the introduction of the euro. This is because, with the introduction of the euro and the dramatically extended geographical reach of the new single unit of account, the scope available to the private sector to enhance the quality of the medium-of-exchange and store-of-value functions of money, where its comparative advantage lies, has been significantly improved. This new and more robust competitive environment should ensure a lively discovery process in the provision of these functions of money as new opportunities are presented for the banking and financial industries in the euro area as a whole.

In the sequence of events on the road to the political integration of Europe, I once had a distinct preference for political union preceding monetary union. As I have argued elsewhere,[31] historical experience shows that national territories and monetary territories normally coincide. Now, of course, the reality is that, if political

---

[30] Such a proposal was advocated at various times by the UK Chancellor and Prime Minister Thatcher as an alternative evolutionary route to monetary union in Europe.

[31] See Otmar Issing, *Europe: Political Union through Common Money*, IEA Occasional Paper 98, February 1996.

[36]

union is ever to occur, monetary union will have preceded it. However, with the establishment of the ECB and the introduction of the single currency, intentionally or not, a process towards further political integration has been triggered. Although this process is not without risks, it nevertheless provides a golden opportunity for Europe to find its proper political shape.

In Hayek's terminology, 'imposing' monetary union on Europe was an act of constructionism. But, to continue with his line of argument, this should also have started a search process for an appropriate political framework so that, finally, the economic and monetary regime and the field of politics together form a viable– if not optimal – institutional arrangement. There are no available patterns from the past which could easily be imitated. Further political integration might subsequently develop in a quite divergent direction. In some areas, more centralisation of decision-making might be necessary, whereas in other fields responsibility might remain, or even be enhanced, at the local, regional or national level.

I have said,[32] and I think it bears repeating, that what is essential for a successful monetary union is a sufficient degree of political commitment by all participating countries, the leading economic actors and the wider public to accept fundamentally and genuinely the political and economic constraints that a single and stable currency represents. The deeper underlying commitment to make European integration a success even in the most difficult of times in history gives some general grounds for hope on this count. Some degree of political unity (not necessarily union), or rather a sense of common responsibility would appear to be important for the long-term health of EMU. However, it is not a substitute for the right economic conditions for lasting success.

---

[32] See Otmar Issing: 'The Euro four weeks after the start', speech delivered at the European-Atlantic Group, House of Commons, London, January 1999.

[37]

Commentary

Lawrence H. White

I AGREE WITH PROFESSOR ISSING that the system of private fiat-type currencies Hayek imagined is probably not 'a viable candidate for a society searching for a stable monetary system.' But I do not wholly agree with him about why this is so. The problem with Hayek's imagined system lies not in legally unrestricted competition among private currencies, as Professor Issing suggests, but only in the irredeemable character Hayek envisions for the currencies. Competition among private issuers in actual practice would be based – and historically always has been based – on a different contractual form, namely demandable debt. Unlike the holder of fiat money, the holder of demandable debt has the option to redeem it. Unlike private fiat money, redeemable private currency is viable and stable. Great merit thus remains in the fundamental message of Hayek's *The Denationalisation of Money*, which is that we should widen the options of money users by removing the legal barriers that restrict competition against central bank currency.

Professor Issing correctly recognises this fundamental message early in his lecture. He notes that *The Denationalisation of Money* was a 'privatisation proposal' that 'called for no less than the abolition of the government's monopoly over the issue of fiat money, leaving the way open for comprehensive competition in its supply by the private sector' (p. 11). Hayek envisioned 'full competition between private issuers of currency'. I am therefore baffled to find Professor Issing later in the lecture claiming that 'What has happened with the introduction of the euro has indeed achieved the denationalisation of money, as advocated by Hayek, at least in the Euro 11 countries.' The truth, of course, is that the European Central Bank (ECB) project does nothing to privatise money. Rather than abolish government monopoly in the supply of fiat money, it actually strengthens the monopoly because it eliminates potential competition among what were the currencies of the eleven member central banks, for example, between the German

[39]

mark and the French franc. What has really happened, as Professor Issing elsewhere recognises, is the supra-nationalisation of money. Supra-nationalisation is certainly not denationalisation as advocated by Hayek.

Professor Issing understands the difference between fiat and redeemable currency. He notes correctly that

> Hayek's proposal must be distinguished from free banking, which refers to a monetary system without a central bank, in which private banks would be allowed to issue currency and bank deposits without restriction. As practised in the 19th century, this version of free banking involved banknotes being redeemable in gold and silver coin (note 6).

I want to suggest that free banking in the sense of competition among redeemable currencies, on a common monetary standard, is the appropriate model for thinking about future private currencies, whether the redemption medium (or 'outside money') is gold or silver coin or something else.

When we focus on a system involving redeemable currency and bank deposits, Professor Issing's principal concerns about currency competition dissolve. Under historical free banking, notes issued by reputable banks normally traded at par against one another, and all traded at par in terms of the (commodity) unit of account. The self-interest of issuers in a competitive system compels them to agree to mutual par acceptance and to pursue policies that maintain it. The problem of a 'multiplicity of exchange rates' that Professor Issing worries about (rightly, with respect to parallel fiat currencies) does not obtain. The same market imperative would ensure that competing issuers maintain 'inter-operability' among private electronic payment instruments. There is no need for central bankers to impose technical standards.

With redeemable rather than irredeemable monies, 'free competition with respect to money' results in a stable and efficient outcome. Redeemability is a 'money-back guarantee' that overcomes the time-inconsistency problem – the temptation to make surprisingly large issues of money in order to gain greater profits – that is a genuine problem with irredeemable currency, public or private, in a world of imperfect foresight.[1] Only in a world of perfect foresight would private fiat issuers not find it more profitable to expand more rapidly. In such a perfect-foresight world, with perfect competition and negligible costs of issue, Professor Issing's conclusion is correct: competition to pay a real return on currency would compel issuers to pursue negative inflation rather than the zero inflation Hayek predicts. It is hard to imagine a model in which currency holders prefer a zero return to a positive return on holding currency.

Professor Issing's critique of *laissez-faire* in money focuses on the 'unit of account' function of money. He rightly reflects that the unit of account 'is a basic convention of society, such as the language and the standards of measurement.' To add an example, a silver standard means that there exists a social convention of posting prices and keeping accounts in units of silver. Pure private enterprise in money is inefficient, Professor Issing suggests, because 'money used as a unit of account has characteristics of a public good'. But how so? A social convention is not *per se* a public good in the standard technical sense. In the standard theory, a public good is something that (absent collective action) is *continually underproduced* because it involves an ongoing cost of production that is in no private party's interest to bear. By contrast, once a convention (a unit of account, language or measurement standard) has been established, *no one needs to keep producing it.* A silver standard will not disappear if tax revenues are not spent to sustain it. Like a language or a measurement standard, it is self-sustaining.

Professor Issing's real concern seems to be that the provision of a *stable purchasing power of the money unit* (rather than merely the provision of a unit as such) is a public good: 'the commitment to maintaining price stability is like the standardisation of units of measurement'. By no means would I wish to deny the importance

---

[1]   On the theory and experience of free banking see George A. Selgin, *The Theory of Free Banking*, Rowman and Littlefield, Totowa, NJ, 1988; Kevin Dowd (ed.), *The Experience of Free Banking*, Routledge, London, 1992; Lawrence H. White, *Free Banking in Britain*, 2nd edn, IEA, 1995. On the contrast with Hayekian competing fiat monies see George Selgin and Lawrence H. White, 'How Would the Invisible Hand Handle Money?' *Journal of Economic Literature*, Vol. 32, December 1994, pp. 1718–49.

of a reliable unit of account for the co-ordination of a decentralised economy. But price stability is not strictly a public good either. Maintaining price stability means maintaining a stable purchasing power for units of outside money. As Professor Issing notes elsewhere, 'outside money provides the unit of account for the whole system'. Stability of purchasing-power is achieved by appropriately matching the quantity of outside money to the quantity demanded. Stable purchasing power is thus a *quality characteristic* of outside money.

Outside money itself is clearly a private good. Accordingly, improvements in its quality – the primary benefits of maintaining a stable purchasing power of money – do not shower down indiscriminately on everyone. They are enjoyed primarily by those who hold the money to which they are attached.

Granted, some benefits of a more stable unit of account may also be enjoyed – apart from money-holding as such – by those who can keep more accurate accounts and make better calculations in such a unit. As Professor Issing puts it, citing Leland Yeager,

> Money with a stable purchasing power serves as the universally acceptable unit of account even for agents who do not use it as a medium of exchange or a store of value (p. 24).

But it seems likely that those who enjoy the largest benefits from a better unit of account – those who have the greatest stake in accurate accounting and calculation – will correspond fairly closely with those who hold the largest outside money balances. If so, then the problem of free-riding on the unit of account is unlikely to be serious. In a competition among outside-money issuers, users would be willing to pay more to hold what they perceive as a higher-quality outside money (or would demand more, at any given price), thus rewarding its producers, who achieve higher revenues. (Professor Issing elsewhere remarks on 'the price people are willing to pay for the use of electronic means of payment'; an analogous notion applies here.) The benefits of high-quality outside money are thus internalised, just as the benefits of providing high quality are internalised with respect to other goods, by the producer enjoying higher prices or larger sales. As Professor Issing notes, such competition goes on to some extent among national fiat currencies today. The relatively widespread use of the Deutsche Mark outside its domestic economy was the Bundesbank's reward for keeping its purchasing power relatively stable.

Hayek imagines that we can rely on such a competition to hold private fiat money issuers to stable purchasing power. The reason that in fact we cannot is the time-consistency problem: as long as people will trade valuable goods and services for his money (in the belief that it will maintain a stable purchasing power), it pays a profit-maximising fiat issuer to print ever more of it.[2] True, over-issue means the loss of the issuer's reputation, but it can be shown that the one-shot profit from a surprisingly large issue generally exceeds the present value of the profit to be gained by staying in business. Potential customers who rightly suspect this will refuse to hold private fiat money in the first place. (Professor Issing points to this very problem when he asks, with respect to a new issuer who promises higher quality, 'why should people be willing to believe the claims of any potential new entrant that its currency will, unlike that of the incumbent(s), turn out to be stable?') For this reason private firms have historically persuaded customers to trust them not by mere promises of stability, but by offering them a money-back contractual guarantee: at any time the customer may redeem the issuer's notes or deposits for outside money.

There is a second major reason to doubt that Hayek's scenario is viable: it envisions multiple units of account operating in parallel within the same economy. Professor Issing is quite right to worry that great inconvenience would occur if there were 'as many *numéraires* as there are issuers'. The advantages of using the same medium of exchange as one's potential trading partners, long ago explained by Carl Menger, drives a network of traders to converge to a common medium of exchange and associated unit of account.[3] Once an outside-money standard has emerged, the disadvantage of

---

[2] Lawrence H. White, *The Theory of Monetary Institutions*, Blackwell, Oxford, 1999.

[3] It is puzzling that Hayek, who edited Menger's collected works, should have overlooked this point in the first edition of *The Denationalisation of Money*. He recognised it in the second edition, but did not revise his imagined system fully enough to obviate the criticism based on it. See Carl Menger, 'On the Origin of Money', *Economic Journal*, Vol. 2, 1892, pp. 239–55 and F. A. Hayek, *The Denationalisation of Money*, 2nd edn, IEA, 1978.

holding a non-par currency or bank account similarly drives money-users to patronise banks that keep their liabilities at par. These forces of convergence to a common standard are akin to other examples of 'network effects,' for example those driving the convergence to a common language, or even to a common video-cassette format. Professor Issing worries, however, about (unspecified) 'network *externalities*' (emphasis added) that 'may inhibit free competition and may make it difficult, if not impossible, to dislodge an incumbent issuer' who misbehaved. He appears to have in mind a situation in which money-users prefer to trade with others using the same unit of account, so that if the established unit of account is *proprietary* (as the private fiat standards imagined by Hayek would be), entry is inhibited.[4] But monetary standards have always been non-proprietary – no one has ever owned exclusive rights to the 'pound of sterling silver' unit of account, for example. When the established monetary unit is *non-proprietary*, the introduction of a new proprietary unit of account is a non-starter and has never been historically observed.

Professor Issing is thus right to stress the greater practical importance of competition in inside (redeemable bank-issued) money. He tells us that national governments

> have not suppressed competition in the supply of … inside money, which has been supplied exclusively by the private sector. Until quite recently, inside money consisted exclusively of bank deposits which were supplied competitively by banks (p. 23).

This statement unfortunately overlooks the fact that, in giving their central banks monopolies of note-issue, governments have suppressed, and continue to suppress, competition in the supply of inside currency or banknotes.[5] Currency is still a significant component of the stock of transactions media (M1), and under

---

4   A proprietary standard, such as the VHS videocassette format, means that intellectual property law prohibits new entrants from conforming to the standard unless they pay a licensing fee.

5   Professor Issing often writes as though 'currency' were synonymous with outside money or high-powered money. Banknotes are currency but are inside money and low-powered money.

competition in the nineteenth century the volume of privately issued banknotes exceeded that of checking deposits.

In a world that admits private banknotes, or their modern electronic counterpart in the form of currency smart cards such as Mondex, we need to amend Professor Issing's statement that

> notes and coins issued by the central bank and, in some cases, by the government are unique in the following sense: they are the only instrument that can mediate a transaction and settle it with finality at one and the same time, by virtue of their status as legal tender (p. 23).

If a payer and recipient agree on payment in banknotes or card balances (issued not by the central bank but by a private commercial bank), then banknotes or card balances settle the transaction with finality. (The recipient has no legal claim against the payer should the issuer go belly-up before the payment is redeemed.) They can do so without having legal tender status. In addition, as Professor Issing himself recognizes, the standard transaction instrument and settlement medium in interbank transactions is not notes and coin, but transferable claims on the clearinghouse bank (in most countries today the central bank). So long as claims on the central bank remain the interbank settlement medium, the unit of central bank liabilities will continue to be demanded and to have a positive value. It will thus be able to serve as the unit of account even if competition from electronic retail payment media were to drive notes and coins out of circulation.

Professor Issing rightly recognises that private competition is today moving the payments system toward greater efficiency. He informs us that the ECB considers certain forms of regulation over private issuers of inside money to be essential for efficiency in the coming electronic payments system, but he provides no argument as to why we need any more than simple enforcement of the contractual arrangements made in a competitive marketplace. Private clearinghouse institutions have historically provided adequate supervision and enforced the redeemability of issuer claims.[6]

---

6   Richard H. Timberlake, 'The Central Banking Rôle of Clearinghouse Associations', *Journal of Money, Credit, and Banking*, Vol. 16, 1984, pp. 1–15.

Particularly baffling from an efficiency standpoint is the ECB demand that central banks be able to 'impose reserve requirements on all issuers of electronic money'. Reserve requirements are nothing but a tax on bank liabilities. They impede rather than enhance the efficiency of the payments system.

Professor Issing says he favours the gradual improvement of the payments system 'by piecemeal engineering,' and rejects 'some abrupt legislative change as sought by proponents of competing currencies and free banking, of which Hayek could, with some justification, be regarded as the high priest'. To be consistent, Professor Issing must then have opposed the abrupt legislative changes by which European monetary union was imposed, of which Jacques Delors could be regarded as the high priest. As he notes, the euro was introduced 'in a 'constructivist' way,' i.e. in 'top-down fashion by legislative decree'. In an earlier era, a consistent Professor Issing would likewise have opposed the legislative changes that introduced central banks and fiat money in the first place.

Hayek himself did not seek abrupt legislative change to overhaul the payments system. He did not even propose to privatise the central bank. He merely proposed to open the field of competition in any country to foreign currencies (in *Choice in Currency*),[7] and then to private currencies (in *The Denationalisation of Money*).[8] Central banks can thus remain in business if, without the benefit of special legal privileges, they can produce a competitive product. I am frankly baffled as to how Professor Issing can suggest that Hayek's proposal to widen freedom of contract, or 'the so-called hard ECU proposal', amounts to dangerous experimentation, but the ECB project does not.

Within the euro zone, Professor Issing tells us, 'any attempt by the private sector to issue banknotes or coins is counterfeiting, a serious criminal offence'. Does this mean that if the UK were to join the euro zone, the banks of Scotland and Northern Ireland would necessarily lose the note-issuing rights that they currently enjoy? Such a restriction could not be squared with the principle of

---

[7] Friedrich A. Hayek, *Choice in Currency*, IEA, 1976.

[8] Friedrich A. Hayek, *The Denationalisation of Money, op. cit.*

subsidiarity, much less with the avoidance of abrupt legislative change to the payments system.

Professor Issing assures us that 'the euro is being managed by a central bank (the ECB) that is protected from political interference by a Treaty' and that its independence 'enables it to pursue its mandated ultimate objective, that is price stability, without interference from government'. Indeed 'monetary independence from political interference and price stability, has, to all intents and purposes, already been achieved'. I believe that such statements are premature at best. It certainly remains to be seen whether the paper safeguards of the Maastricht Treaty will prove durable and the objective of 'price stability' will long remain uncompromised. No tangible enforcement mechanism binds the ECB to its mandate, and nothing prevents the ECB governing council from deciding that the somewhat ambiguous phrase 'price stability' means something other than its current interpretation, consumer price inflation of less than 2% over the medium term. We should remember that when the Federal Reserve System began, its supporters claimed that the structure of the system rendered its operations independent from government (indeed, made it not even a central bank). A generation later the claim could not be seriously maintained.

Commentary

Roland Vaubel

OTMAR ISSING IS OPPOSED TO COMPETITION from private suppliers of currencies (outside money) because he believes it to be 'inefficient'. He prefers the state monopoly. In an earlier lecture, however, he welcomed international currency competition among central banks.[1] This is puzzling. If the forces of competition are useful in constraining public suppliers of money, would they not also be effective in constraining private ones? It is this reasoning that led Hayek from *Choice in Currency* to *The Denationalisation of Money*.

Issing presents a long list of objections to Hayek's proposal. None of them is new, and none has escaped severe criticism in the literature. It is a pity that Issing does not seem to know the objections to the objections or that he does not bother to deal with them. He might have raised the discussion to a higher level.

Issing's first objection is that currency competition would lead to deflation:

> In the context of the type of competition envisaged by Hayek, the nominal rate of interest would be driven (close) to zero ... It would, therefore, appear that the outcome earnestly desired by Hayek, a money of stable value, would not be achieved in practice by his own proposal of competing currencies (pp. 13, 18).

This conclusion is premature. Money is not only an asset but also a standard of value. If the users of money prefer a stable standard of value, they might be willing to forego a positive rate of return on banknotes and coins. Deflation, it is true, is a possibility but so is price level stability. As Milton Friedman has argued, we do not know which one is optimal. That is why we need (potential)

---

[1] Otmar Issing, 'Hayek's Suggestion for Currency Competition: A Central Banker's View', in Stephen F. Frowen (ed.), *Hayek: Economist and Social Philosopher*, Macmillan, Basingstoke, 1997, pp. 185–93.

competition and choice. To predict deflation, as Issing does, is, in Hayek's words, a 'pretence of knowledge'. Hayek, it is true, expressed the expectation that competitive money would be stable. But he did not pretend to know it, for

> the government monopoly of issuing money has not only deprived us of good money but has also deprived us of the only *process* by which we can find out what good money is.[2]

Second, Issing objects that 'network externalities also provide a rationale for regulation' (p. 18). The fact that the use of money gives rise to network externalities is not in dispute, and Hayek, too, was aware of it. But does it justify government regulation or a state monopoly? Positive externalities may warrant subsidies. Regulation is inferior because the government does not know the suppliers' cost function. But it might not even know what the externalities are. If the government regulates the standard of value, that is, if it imposes a common standard of value, it may not only pick the wrong common standard – it would also overlook the possibility that different users may prefer different standards. Each user prefers a standard that is stable in terms of his or her basket of goods and services. As different individuals and groups of individuals (regions, countries) consume different baskets of goods and services, they may also prefer different standards of value. That is how, in the regions of China, a silver and a copper standard competed side by side at flexible exchange rates for 200 years.[3] Of course, the government may propose a standard of value ('open regulation'). But it should not impose it.

What about network externalities in the use of media of exchange? When choosing between different means of payments, each user of money internalises a large part of the transaction costs. That is why he has a strong incentive to choose the medium of

---

[2] Friedrich A. von Hayek, 'Toward a Free-Market Monetary System', in James A. Dorn and Anna Schwartz (eds.), *The Search for Stable Money*, Chicago University Press, Chicago 1987, pp. 383–90.

[3] Chau-nan Chen, 'Flexible Bimetallic Exchange Rates in China, 1650–1850 – A Historical Example of Optimum Currency Areas', *Journal of Money, Credit and Banking*, Vol. 7, 1975, pp. 359–76.

exchange which also minimises the transaction costs of his trading partners, the external cost. There is a type of 'invisible hand' process at work. If the network effect turned out to be dominant, the market would – as in the case of a natural monopoly – converge to a single monetary standard and means of payment. Such a monopolist, it is true, might have to be regulated. But without free entry for competitors, we do not know whether a single money is optimal, and as history shows, currency competition may not destroy itself.

Yet Issing goes beyond the normal externality case. He claims, thirdly, that there is a public good problem:

[Hayek's] recommendation neglected the 'public good' aspect of money, which derives from its function as a unit of account … The purely private provision of a public good (the unit-of-account function of money) would, in this case, be suboptimal (pp. 24, 18).

If this were the case, there would be a danger of underproduction. To overcome underproduction, however, it is neither necessary nor helpful to give the government the right of monopoly.

Standards of value – such as price indices and stock market indices – meet the non-rivalry test, and exclusion is costly. Nevertheless, many of them are privately produced – usually in conjunction with some private good. Money as a unit of account, too, is jointly produced with money as a means of payment, which is a private good. Any monetary means of payment is necessarily denominated in a unit of account. Money as a unit of account is also jointly consumed or used with money as a means of payment. If the public prefers a stable standard of value, it will also prefer the means of payment that is denominated in a stable standard of value. The stability of the public good 'monetary standard' raises the demand for the private good 'monetary means of payment'. That is why, in practice, the producers of money have a sufficient incentive to supply a stable standard of value.

Issing's fourth objection relates to the problem of time inconsistency:

how could one be sure that … the private issuer would not then, in a time-inconsistent fashion that has become all too familiar under politically dependent central banks, start to engage in inflationary overissue so as to maximise seigniorage? (p. 17)

In his 1997 lecture, which has already been mentioned, he even firmly asserts that

> there will always be an incentive for the suppliers of money to break ex post their original promise regarding the purchasing power movement of their own money.[4]

Issing adds, 'The assumption of complete, symmetric and free information implicitly assumed in the Hayek proposal does not apply to banking' (p. 18). Did Hayek – here or anywhere else – assume 'complete information'?

The danger of time-inconsistent behaviour does, of course, exist in the field of money production – regardless of whether the money is issued by a central bank or a private bank. However, as in the standard literature on the time-inconsistency problem,[5] the users of money will rationally expect such cheating. They will demand value guarantees, and competition will force the private suppliers to satisfy this demand. As Hayek pointed out, it is difficult to predict what the backing would look like. It could be gold, commodities, equity, financial assets or even the money issued by some other, dominant supplier (a 'private currency board'). Once more, competition would be needed as a discovery procedure. But Hayek clearly assumes that the issuers would have to back up their promises. As in the Scottish free banking system, redemption would not have to be immediate. But the issuers would have to be liable with their property.

Finally, Issing expresses the fear that

> competing private issuers would decide to collude by fixing the relative values of their currencies ... if some arrangement were to be arrived at by private issuers to counter the tendency for the values of the different monies to fluctuate against each other, then the bad money would drive out the good money ... In other words, Gresham's law would, most likely, start to apply (p. 20).

---

[4]   Issing, 1997, *op. cit.*, p. 192.

[5]   For example, Robert J. Barro and David B. Gordon, 'A Positive Theory of Monetary Policy in a Natural Rate Model', *Journal of Political Economy*, Vol. 91, 1983, pp. 589–610.

The danger of collusion is present in any private market. We do not usually regard it as a sufficient reason to establish a government monopoly. There are better ways of dealing with this danger. The unilateral fixing of an exchange rate does not imply collusion. As the European Monetary System has shown, it is not the end of competition. Nor does the fixing of exchange rates as such invoke Gresham's law. As Hayek has pointed out (in a passage quoted by Issing!), Gresham's law does not operate unless the fixed exchange rate is a forced exchange rate. But private issuers cannot impose an exchange rate on creditors. Only governments can do that.

Issing is fully aware that the European money monopoly which the European Union has just established and which Otmar Issing serves as a central banker, 'is virtually the opposite of what Hayek proposed'. But Issing argues that 'the process towards further political integration', which he believes to be triggered by monetary union, 'provides a golden opportunity for Europe to find its proper political shape' (p. 37). Would Hayek, like Issing, regard further political integration, that is, centralisation, as a golden opportunity? In *The Constitution of Liberty*, Hayek notes that

> while it has also been characteristic of those favouring an increase in governmental powers to support maximum concentration of power, those mainly concerned with individual liberty have generally advocated decentralisation.[6]

Hayek was mainly concerned with individual liberty and firmly opposed to centralisation.

---

6 Friedrich A. von Hayek, *The Constitution of Liberty*, Routledge & Kegan Paul, London, 1960, p. 263.

Afterword

Otmar Issing

---

1 Rejoinder to Professor White

I AM GRATEFUL FOR PROFESSOR WHITE'S CAREFUL ANALYSIS. I am grateful also for the opportunity to clarify some of the issues, at least one of which may derive from a confusion of language.

There is an issue which coloured virtually all of Hayek's thinking and which, I think, might not be sufficiently stressed by Professor White. It is worth re-emphasising. At least according to my reading of Hayek, he found the prevailing monetary arrangements, at the time when he was writing, so deplorably prone to inflation that virtually anything else would have been preferable. Arrangements based on competing private monies would, he thought, have been better and this is a view for which I have some sympathy. Arguably, Hayek's overriding concern centred on the belief that inflation was a 'monetary evil' which was inflicted on the ordinary person by the government's monopoly of money. People were effectively being cheated by the existing monetary arrangements by having their savings systematically eroded and price signals systematically distorted by inflation. But these abuses are also the central concerns of every honest central banker. After a long experience and, I would surmise, particularly that of the inflationary 1970s, Hayek may have despaired of the possibility of reforming the existing system. My earnest judgement and my sincerest hope, is that events since then have proved him wrong. I think these have shown that the existing system is capable of reforming itself. It can, and it has done so to a substantial extent. Ironically, it has done so to some extent in a way which Hayek had advocated in his earlier writings.

One cannot neglect the important progress that has been made since Hayek published his seminal contribution in *The Denationalisation of Money*. In Europe, to take the case with which I am most immediately concerned, and as I indicated in my paper, all of the constituent National Central Banks (NCBs) in the Eurosystem, as well as the European Central Bank (ECB) itself, are now fully politically independent and, according to their respective statutes, cannot take instructions from governments of the member states. The ECB now has a clear mandate derived from the Maastricht Treaty to maintain price stability. The separation between public finance and monetary policy is further guaranteed by the Treaty prohibition on monetary financing of the public sector or privileged access to funding from financial institutions. In my view, these are very important and substantial reforms which Hayek, in his later writings, thought were not politically feasible.

However, it is far too early to judge whether these reforms are going to be a lasting success or not. I agree with Professor White that claims of success based merely on Treaty provisions could turn out to be premature. And indeed it does remain to be seen whether the safeguards of the Maastricht Treaty prove to be durable and the constitutional objective of price stability uncompromised. All the ECB can do is everything that is in its power to respect its obligations under the Treaty. It should also be emphasised that we may not have reached the end of the line with reform of the monetary system. The history of thinking about, and of implementing, institutional arrangements has probably not ended with the implementation of the Maastricht Treaty.

One of the main concerns I expressed about the Hayek scheme has to do with the risks and practical difficulties associated with its implementation. But is not the Maastricht Treaty also a leap into the dark which, according to Professor White, I should have opposed because it involved an abrupt legislative change of the type that would also have been required to implement the Hayek scheme? Well, yes and no. True, the Maastricht Treaty ushers in a monetary arrangement unprecedented anywhere, or at any time, in the world to date. It implies a regime change reflected in the introduction of a new currency, in the lifting of monetary policy to a new supra-national level and in rendering the whole of the Eurosystem legally independent of political interference. However, there is also a very large element of continuity with the monetary framework which, as formulated and operated by the Bundesbank, had delivered widely admired results.

There may be a degree of linguistic imprecision in my use of the word 'denationalisation'. I am well aware, of course, that 'supra-nationalisation' was not exactly the concept that Hayek had in mind when talking about denationalisation. More specifically, the word 'denationalisation' in my paper was not intended to mean 'privatisation'. It was intended to mean that arbitrary interference by national governments in the management of money has been eliminated in the euro area. It has been denationalised in the sense that money is taken out of the control of national governments and, at the same time, 'supra-nationalised' by being brought to an international level. Neither of those moves involves any element of privatisation, of course.

As Professor White correctly points out, the distinction between redeemable and irredeemable issue is of central importance. However, I am not so sure that systems based on redeemability can have the ironclad guarantee that Professor White seems to imply. Take the case where the balance sheet of an issuer is hit by a large negative shock, which brings into question the issuer's solvency. Its note issue will start to trade at a discount. More generally, there is no guarantee that the holders of the currencies issued by different issuers would not start to differentiate their value depending on their perceptions of the riskiness of the respective portfolios. It is therefore far from certain that multiple units of account would not emerge even if redeemability is promised.

Professor White agrees with me in stressing the greater practical importance of competition in inside money but says I overlook the fact that governments have suppressed competition in inside currency. The restriction relates to the freedom to supply analogue notes and coin. But there is no prohibition, although there are some regulations to be respected, as indicated in my paper, in the supply of the electronic equivalent of analogue notes and coin – that is, electronic money. Given that electronic money, along with other electronically-based retail payments media, are potentially much more efficient than analogue money, the current prohibition on the issue of analogue notes and coin by private issuers can scarcely any longer be said to be an enormous burden on the private sector's participation in the supply of payments media, although it may have been in the past. The scope for private commercial opportunity in supplying analogue currency is now very limited given that, for example, in the US, currency (adjusted for estimated holdings outside the US) comprises only about 1% of the wide money stock.

I would just like to note in passing that Professor White ought not to be unduly baffled by one of the regulations relating to the issue of electronic money, namely the imposition of reserve requirements. This is because required reserves in the Eurosystem are remunerated at a rate of interest corresponding to the average rate of the ECB's weekly tenders over the maintenance period for reserve requirements; that is, in effect, close to the market rate of interest. The tax element is therefore minimal.

2 Rejoinder to Professor Vaubel

I thank Professor Vaubel for his comments. He recommends that the government should confine itself to proposing standards of value but not imposing such standards. But I, like some of those I quote in my paper, consider a standard of value to be very much like a standard of measurement. And, of course, governments do prohibit competing units of measurement and with good reason. I think the outcome would be chaotic if the private sector were to start using a whole array of new units of measurement competing with the centimetre, the metre and the kilometre.

Hayek, as correctly noted by Vaubel, expressed the expectation that competitive money would be stable but that he did not pretend to know it. The reason why he did not know it is because the government monopoly of money has 'deprived us of the only process by which we can find out what good money is'. Those who would espouse the teachings of Hayek would therefore appear to advocate experimenting with the economy. Their position would seem to be that there is no way that we can be sure in advance what would happen if the government were to rescind its monopoly status as supplier of currency, but let us have a go anyway. Let us see what would happen when the Hayekian discovery process, driven by uninhibited private market competition, is given free rein. Should not any reasonable person have doubts about the workability and the ultimate outcome of the Hayekian process in practice? Vaubel himself can only say that such 'currency competition *may not* destroy itself' [emphasis added]. One would therefore have to be sceptical of such a call for experimentation.

[58]

3 Final remark

No doubt, given my current position as an Executive Board member of the ECB, Professors Vaubel and White will both see me as biased in defending the 'state monopoly money' model. They may indeed be correct in their perceptions. From an intellectual perspective, I find Hayek's philosophy of 'competition as a discovery process' appealing. However, as someone responsible for concrete monetary policy actions, it behoves me to be at least rather conservative if not risk averse. Therefore, I clearly cannot discuss Hayek's proposal only from a purely intellectual perspective despite the fact that I still am, as I always have been, very interested in monetary theory. I am forced, as a practical central banker, to make a judgement on the best way to proceed. Minimising the risk to money and the related risk to the stability of the overall financial system and, as history demonstrates, the more broadly related risks to society in general, is at the heart of my concerns.

THE ANNUAL IEA HAYEK
MEMORIAL LECTURES*

1988	The Rt Hon. Nigel Lawson MP	Chancellor of the Exchequer	The State of the Market
1989	The Rt Hon. Robin Leigh-Pemberton	Governor of the Bank of England	The Future of Monetary Arrangements in Europe
1990	Dr Karl Otto Pöhl	President, Deutsche Bundesbank	Two Monetary Unions – The Bundesbank's View
1992	Professor Jeffrey Sachs	Harvard University	Privatisation in Eastern Europe
1993	Professor Michael Novak	American Enterprise Institute	Two Moral Ideals of Business
1994	Dr Peter D. Sutherland	Director General, GATT	A New Framework for International Economic Relations
1995	The Rt Hon. Francis Maude	Morgan Stanley and Chairman of the Government's De-regulation Task Force	State and Society: Restoring the Balance
1996	Dr Donald T. Brash	Governor, Reserve Bank of New Zealand	New Zealand's Remarkable Reforms
1997	Professor Ing. Vaclav Klaus	Prime Minister of the Czech Republic	The Transformation of Czech Society: Retrospect and Prospect
1998	Professor Jonathan Sacks	The Chief Rabbi	Morals and Markets
1999	Professor Otmar Issing	Member, Executive Board of the European Central Bank	Hayek, Currency Competition and European Monetary Union

* The Title 'Hayek Memorial Lecture' was applied to this Public Lecture Series from 1992 onwards.

Morals and Markets

Professor Jonathan Sacks' 1998 IEA Hayek Memorial Lecture on Morals and Markets was generally regarded as one of the most stimulating contributions to this subject in recent years. The Institute therefore commissioned three other distinguished authors to write commentaries on Professor Sacks' paper. The four papers are published in this volume, together with an Afterword by Professor Sacks.

Contents

The Institute of Economic Affairs
2 Lord North Street, Westminster, London SW1P 3LB
Telephone: 0171 799 3745 Facsimile: 0171 799 2137
E-mail: iea@iea.org.uk Internet: http://www.iea.org.uk   ISBN 0-255 36424-

£6.00

Privatisation, Competition and Regulation

Stephen C. Littlechild

1. Austrian economists regard utilities as exceptional cases where regulation may be justified.

2. The long term aim for a public utility should be to '...turn as much as possible of that industry into a private, competitive and unregulated industry'. In the short term this may mean a 'considerable role for regulation'.

3. Price cap (RPI-X) regulation gives better efficiency incentives to companies than traditional US regulation and passes benefits on to consumers.

4. UK style privatisation and regulation put competition at the forefront whereas '...traditional US regulation for the most part suppressed it.'

5. In electricity, competition in generation has stimulated efficiency improvements but it is still not fully effective.

6. Big generators still set wholesale prices most of the time and the government's 'stricter consents' policy for gas-fired plant hinders entry to generation: that policy is the 'most significant obstacle to a more competitive market'.

7. Competition to supply industrial consumers has resulted in large numbers of companies switching to new suppliers and prices have fallen considerably.

8. Introducing competition to supply domestic consumers was a major logistical exercise. The cost was more than justified by the lower prices and other benefits now flowing from competition.

9. Some of the changes to utility regulation now proposed by the government will not be helpful - such as the qualification to the regulators' duty to promote competition.

10. The next step should be a further transfer, from government to consumers, of control over the utilities. A challenge is to find ways by which competition can substitute for regulation in remaining monopoly sectors.

The Institute of Economic Affairs

2 Lord North Street, Westminster, London SW1P 3LB
Telephone: 0171 799 3745 Facsimile: 0171 799 2137
E-mail: iea@iea.org.uk Internet: http://www.iea.org.uk   ISBN 0-255 36480-6

£5.00

What Price Civil Justice?

Brian Main and Alan Peacock
With a Commentary by Bruce Benson

1. In Britain the costs of justice - to taxpayers and litigants - have been rising faster than GDP.
2. For efficiency reasons and to encourage innovation, reform is required and some action is already underway.
3. But reform is complicated because 'justice' is a complex product - bought on 'trust' by many consumers and with precedent and spillover effects.
4. Some good ideas for reform are already in circulation. But there is a case for experimentation rather than trying to work out in advance which ideas should be implemented.
5. Market forces should have a bigger role in the civil justice system and there should be more competition in the provision of dispute resolution services.
6. Probable features of a reformed judicial system would be competitive tendering, better information for clients about alternative ways of proceeding and more power for trial judges to control the passage of a case.
7. The supply of judges also needs to be addressed: court fees could be determined by market forces and the proceeds ploughed back into judicial capacity.
8. Alternative dispute resolution (ADR) procedures allow parties a choice of jurisdictions.
9. ADR produces precedents, to the extent they are required, and does not need the threat of litigation in the background.
10. A big advantage of ADR is that it avoids monopolized law which otherwise tends to produce inflexibility, bad rules and politicization.

The Institute of Economic Affairs
2 Lord North Street, Westminster, London SW1P 3LB
Telephone: 0171 799 3745 Facsimile: 0171 799 2137
E-mail: iea@iea.org.uk Internet: http://www.iea.org.uk   ISBN 0-255 36429-6

£8.00